5/06

PRAIRIE FOOD CHAINS

Kelley MacAulay & Bobbie Kalman
Crabtree Publishing Company
www.crabtreebooks.com

Created by Bobbie Kalman

Dedicated by Arlene Arch-Wilson
For my two special loves, Logan and Darrien. You take my breath away.
Love Aunt Eenie

Editor-in-Chief
Bobbie Kalman

Writing team
Kelley MacAulay
Bobbie Kalman

Substantive editor
Kathryn Smithyman

Editors
Molly Aloian
Kristina Lundblad

Design
Katherine Kantor

Cover design and series logo
Samantha Crabtree

Production coordinator
Katherine Kantor

Photo research
Crystal Foxton

Consultant
Patricia Loesche, Ph.D., Animal Behavior Program,
Department of Psychology, University of Washington

Illustrations
Barbara Bedell: pages 3 (badger, mouse, rabbit, rat, raven and squirrel),
    8 (wolf), 9 (weasel, rabbit, ants, mouse and rat), 14, 16, 25 (all except
    earthworm), 27 (owl and mouse), 30, 31 (pencils)
Katherine Kantor: pages 5, 27 (fox), 31 (magazine cover)
Jeannette McNaughton-Julich: pages 15, 22
Margaret Amy Reiach: series logo illustration, pages 3 (butterflies, flowers,
    and plant), 7 (all except eagle), 8 (prairie dog), 9 (butterfly and all
    plants except 4th from left), 10 (sun), 11, 12, 25 (earthworm),
    27 (plant, prairie dog, and grasses)
Bonna Rouse: pages 3 (eagle), 7 (eagle), 8 (plant) 9 (eagle and plant-4th
    from left), 10 (plant)

Photographs
Visuals Unlimited: Steve Maslowski: page 23
Other images by Corbis, Corel, Digital Stock, Digital Vision, Eyewire,
    and Otto Rogge Photography

Crabtree Publishing Company

www.crabtreebooks.com   1-800-387-7650

Cataloging-in-Publication Data
MacAulay, Kelley.
    Prairie food chains / Kelley MacAulay & Bobbie Kalman.
        p. cm. -- (The food chains series)
    Includes index.
    ISBN-13: 978-0-7787-1947-2 (RLB)
    ISBN-10: 0-7787-1947-2 (RLB)
    ISBN-13: 978-0-7787-1993-9 (pbk.)
    ISBN-10: 0-7787-1993-6 (pbk.)
    1. Prairie ecology--Juvenile literature. 2. Food chains (Ecology)--
Juvenile literature. I. Kalman, Bobbie. II. Title.
    QH541.5.P7M33 2005
    577.4'416--dc22
                                                            2005000488
                                                            LC

**Published in
the United States**
PMB16A
350 Fifth Ave.
Suite 3308
New York, NY
10118

**Published
in Canada**
616 Welland Ave.,
St. Catharines, Ontario
Canada
L2M 5V6

**Published in the
United Kingdom**
73 Lime Walk
Headington
Oxford
OX3 7AD
United Kingdom

**Published
in Australia**
386 Mt. Alexander Rd.,
Ascot Vale (Melbourne)
VIC 3032

Contents

What are prairies?

Prairies are wide, flat areas of land where many types of tall grasses grow. Prairies stretch down the middle of North America, from the southern part of Canada to the southern part of the United States.

Prairie weather

Summers in the prairies are warm, but winters are very cold. Prairies usually receive about 10 to 30 inches (25-76 cm) of rain and snow per year. Between rainfalls, there are often **droughts**. Droughts are periods of time when little rain falls. Few trees grow in prairies because trees cannot grow in areas where droughts occur.

Bull elk, such as the one shown above, are large animals that feed on prairie grasses. Many other kinds of animals also live and feed in prairies.

4

Types of prairies

There are three types of prairies in North America—**tallgrass prairies**, **shortgrass prairies**, and **mixed-grass prairies**. Each type of prairie has grasses that grow to different heights. In tallgrass prairies, grasses can grow to be over five feet (1.5 m) high! In shortgrass prairies, grasses grow up to only about two feet (0.6 m) high. Mixed-grass prairies have areas with tall grasses and areas with short grasses.

Prairie land is flat, so prairies can be windy places!

Where do prairies grow?

Tallgrass prairies grow in the eastern part of North America, where more rain falls. Shortgrass prairies grow in the western part of North America, where there is less rain. Mixed-grass prairies grow between shortgrass prairies and tallgrass prairies.

The map on the right shows where each type of prairie grows in North America.

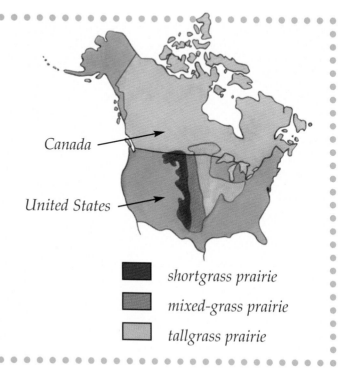

Canada

United States

■ shortgrass prairie
■ mixed-grass prairie
■ tallgrass prairie

What is a food chain?

This ground squirrel gets nutrients and energy by eating grasses and insects.

There are many living things on Earth. Some living things are plants, and others are animals. Plants and animals are different, but they need the same things to stay alive. Both need air, water, sunlight, and food.

Energy from food

Plants and animals receive two important things from food—**nutrients** and **energy**. Plants and animals need nutrients to stay healthy. Plants need energy to grow and to make new plants. Animals need energy to move, to breathe air, to find food, and to grow.

The sun's energy

Plants and animals get energy in different ways. Plants make food, whereas animals eat food. To make food, plants use energy from the sun.

Food for animals

Different animals eat different kinds of food. Some animals eat plants. Others eat the animals that feed on plants. Some animals eat both plants and animals! The pattern that is created when animals eat plants and other animals to get food energy is called a **food chain**. To see how a food chain works, look at the diagram on the right.

Energy from the sun

Green plants trap the sun's energy and use it to make food. They use some of the energy as food and store the rest.

sun

plant

When an animal such as a prairie dog eats a plant, it gets only the amount of energy that was stored in the plant. The prairie dog does not get as much of the sun's energy as the plant received.

prairie dog

eagle

When an eagle eats a prairie dog, energy is passed to the eagle through the prairie dog. The eagle gets less of the sun's energy than the amount the prairie dog received.

Levels in a food chain

There are three levels in a food chain. Plants make up the first level. The second level is made up of animals that eat plants. Animals that eat other animals make up the third level.

Making food

Plants are **primary producers**. They are the **primary**, or first, living things in a food chain. Plants **produce**, or make, their own food. The food plants do not use is stored as energy.

Eating plants

Herbivores are animals that eat plants. They make up the second level of a food chain. Herbivores are called **primary consumers**. Primary consumers are the first group of living things that must **consume**, or eat, food to survive. They receive some of the sun's energy that is stored in plants.

Eating meat

The third level of a food chain is made up of **carnivores**. Carnivores eat other animals. They are also called **secondary consumers**. In a food chain, they are the second group of living things that must eat to get energy from food. When carnivores eat herbivores or other carnivores, they get less of the sun's energy than plants or the other animals get.

8

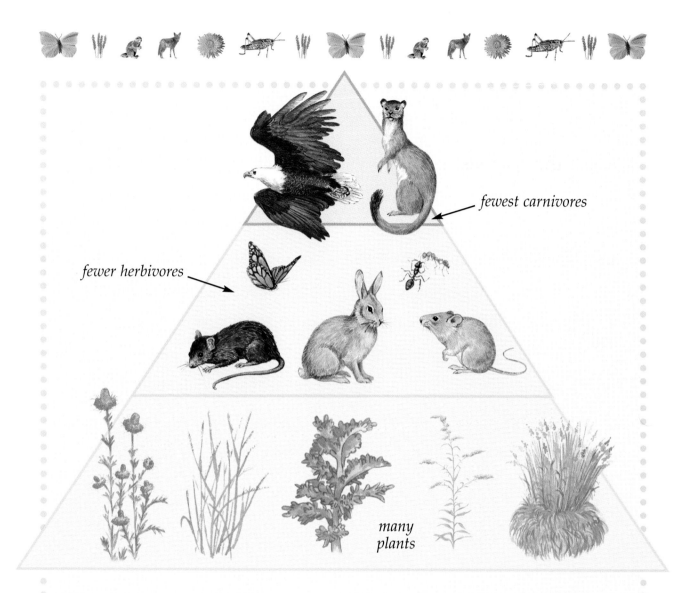

fewest carnivores

fewer herbivores

many plants

The energy pyramid

This pyramid shows the movement of energy in a food chain. A pyramid is wide at the bottom and narrow at the top. The first level of the energy pyramid is wide because there are many plants. Many plants are needed to make enough food energy for animals. The second level is narrower because there are fewer herbivores than there are plants. There are fewer herbivores because each one must eat many plants. The top level of the pyramid is the narrowest because there are fewer carnivores than there are plants or herbivores. Carnivores must eat many herbivores to get the food energy they need.

Making food

Only plants can make their own food using sunlight. Making food using sunlight is called **photosynthesis**. Plants contain **chlorophyll**, which is a green **pigment**, or color. Chlorophyll **absorbs**, or takes in, energy from the sun.

To make food, chlorophyll combines the sun's energy with water and **carbon dioxide**. Carbon dioxide is a gas that is a part of air. The food plants make is a type of sugar called **glucose**. Plants use some glucose as energy and store the rest.

Helpful plants

Plants are helpful to animals. Plants remove carbon dioxide from the air as they make food. Too much carbon dioxide is harmful to animals. Plants also release **oxygen** into the air. Animals need to breathe the oxygen plants release.

A plant takes in nutrients and water from the soil through its roots. A prairie plant has long roots that can reach water deep in the soil during droughts.

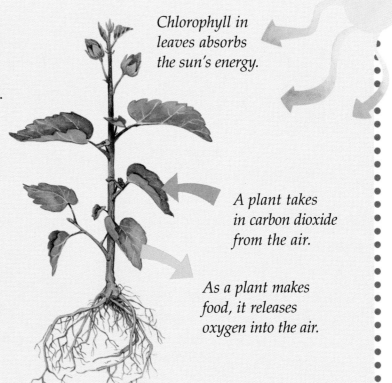

Chlorophyll in leaves absorbs the sun's energy.

A plant takes in carbon dioxide from the air.

As a plant makes food, it releases oxygen into the air.

Prairie plants

Many types of plants grow in prairies. Two common plants in tallgrass prairies are big bluestem grass and Indian grass. Both are important sources of food for bison. Purple prairie clover grows in shortgrass prairies. This plant has many of the nutrients that animals need to stay healthy.

Indian grass

Fire!

During droughts, prairie plants become dry and can catch fire easily. Fires are good for prairies, however! Fires burn only the tops of prairie plants. The roots of the plants remain healthy, so the plants can keep growing. Fire turns the tops of the plants into ash, which falls into the soil. Ash adds many nutrients to the soil. The added nutrients help new prairie plants grow.

big bluestem grass   *purple prairie clover*

Prairie plant-eaters

There is a lot of food for plant-eating animals in prairies! Many prairie herbivores eat different plants every day to get the nutrients they need.

Plant foods

Most prairie herbivores are **grazers**. Grazers eat grasses and other small plants that grow near the ground. As grazers eat, they bite off the tops of the grasses, making the grasses shorter. When prairie grasses are short, more sunlight can reach the soil, which helps new plants grow. Other prairie herbivores are **browsers**. Browsers eat leafy plants, shoots, shrubs, and twigs.

Mule deer are browsers. They eat shrubs, such as the fringed sage shown right.

Prairie plant foods

Different herbivores eat different plant parts. Many birds, bees, and butterflies feed on **nectar**, which is a sweet liquid found in flowers. Black-eyed Susans, shown right, are common prairie flowers that provide nectar for birds and butterflies. Some birds also eat seeds. Small animals, such as ground squirrels, eat leaves, seeds, and fruits.

This bee is feeding on nectar.

13

Prairie dogs

Prairies are important **habitats** for many animals. A habitat is the natural place where an animal lives. Prairie dogs are animals that live only in prairies. They are herbivores that feed on tall grasses. Prairie dogs are important animals in prairie food chains. They are eaten by many carnivores.

*Prairie dogs are not actually dogs! They are **rodents**. Rodents are animals with long front teeth that never stop growing. Prairie dogs are called "dogs" because they sometimes make barking noises to warn one another of danger.*

Prairie dog towns

Prairie dogs live in groups. They build large underground homes called **towns**. Prairie dog towns have many rooms that are connected by tunnels. Prairie dogs use different rooms in different ways. For example, they eat in some rooms and store food in others.

The towns even have sleeping rooms, where prairie dogs **hibernate**, or sleep through the winter. The underground rooms stay warm during the cold winter months. During times of heavy rain, prairie dogs pile dirt around the entrance to each tunnel. The dirt stops water from flooding into the town.

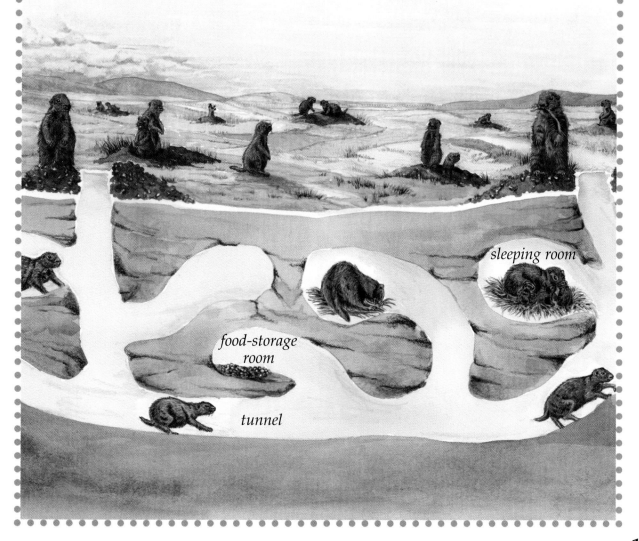

sleeping room

food-storage room

tunnel

Roaming bison

Bison are large herbivores that live in groups called **herds**. Bison are grazers that eat prairie grasses. In the early 1800s, there were millions of bison roaming on prairies! As more people moved into prairie lands, they began killing the bison. By the late 1800s, almost all the bison were killed. People killed some of the bison for food, but most were killed for their shaggy fur. Bison fur was often sold for a lot of money.

As more people moved into prairie lands, they built railways across the land. Hunters rode trains into prairies to find and hunt bison. Some people killed bison for sport.

Changing food chains

Bison are important parts of prairie food chains. Carnivores such as mountain lions eat bison. When people killed too many bison, there was not enough food for carnivores.

More bison

By the 1900s, people began to realize how important bison were. They created **national parks**, where bison could live safely and have babies. National parks are natural areas protected by governments. Over time, the number of bison began to grow again. Today, there are thousands of bison living in national parks throughout prairie lands.

Prairie predators

The black-footed ferret is a secondary consumer. It feeds mainly on prairie dogs, which are herbivores.

Many of the carnivores that live in prairies are **predators**. Predators are animals that hunt other animals. The animals predators hunt are called **prey**. Predators are secondary consumers when they hunt and eat herbivores. Some predators are also **tertiary consumers**. "Tertiary" means "third." Tertiary consumers eat secondary consumers, so they are the third group of animals in a food chain.

Hungry hawks

The red-tailed hawk is a common predator in prairies. It is both a secondary consumer and a tertiary consumer. This hawk is a secondary consumer when it eats a herbivore such as a prairie dog. When it eats another carnivore, such as a snake, the red-tailed hawk is a tertiary consumer.

Helpful hunters

Prairie herbivores eat a lot of plants! Predators, such as the cougar shown below, help control the **populations** of animals that eat prairie plants. Without predators, there would be too many herbivores and soon all the prairie plants would be eaten. Predators also help keep herds of different herbivores healthy. Predators hunt the young, sick, or old animals in a herd. Without these weak animals in the herd, the healthy animals have more food.

Cougars live mainly in forests, but they often leave the forests to hunt mule deer, pronghorns, white-tailed deer, and young bison in prairies.

19

Staying alive

Prairie land is flat, so predators can see prey animals from far away. The bodies of many prairie animals have **adapted**, or changed, so that the animals can survive in the open spaces. Some animals stay alive by blending in, whereas other animals escape predators by running fast.

The pronghorn is the fastest land animal in North America! Running fast helps the pronghorn escape predators such as cougars and wolves. Pronghorns also have large eyes, which help them watch for predators.

Catching prey

Some predators work together to catch large animals, such as bison. Wolves hunt as a group. They begin a hunt by chasing a herd of bison. As the herd runs away, the young, sick, or old bison fall behind the rest of the herd. These animals fall behind because they cannot run as fast as the stronger animals in the herd. The wolves then surround one of the slow-moving bison and attack it.

Bison are large, strong animals. It may take a group of wolves a few days to kill a bison.

Prairie omnivores

Some prairie animals are **omnivores**. Omnivores are animals that survive by eating both plants and animals. Meadowlarks, wild turkeys, and skunks are prairie omnivores.

skunk

Omnivores are also known as **opportunistic feeders**. Opportunistic feeders are animals that eat whichever foods are available to them. They rarely go hungry because they have many foods from which to choose!

This badger is an omnivore. It eats fruits, seeds, grasses, prairie dogs, and ground squirrels. A badger even eats venomous rattlesnakes! Venomous snakes have poison in their bodies.

Seasonal foods

Prairie omnivores cannot eat the same foods throughout the year. Their **diets**, or the foods they eat, change as the seasons change. Omnivores change their diets because many of the foods they eat in summer are not available in winter. In winter, small plants are often buried under snow and the animals that eat them must find different plants to eat. Some animals hibernate in winter. Hibernating animals do not eat, and they are not eaten by other animals. While animals hibernate, they are not part of food chains.

Prairie chickens are omnivores that live only in prairies. In summer, their diets are made up of plant foods and insects. In winter, when insects are hard to find, prairie chickens eat the tops of tall grasses, which stick out of the snow.

Recycling nutrients

When animals die, their bodies still contain nutrients. **Scavengers**, such as the red fox above, are animals that eat **carrion**, or dead animals, to get the leftover nutrients. If scavengers did not eat carrion, the nutrients would be wasted. Scavengers do not eat all of the carrion, however! The parts of dead animals that scavengers do not eat are eaten by **decomposers** such as worms or snails. Decomposers are living things that eat and break down the leftover bits of dead plants and animals.

Both scavengers and decomposers help keep prairies clean. Without them, dead plants and animals would pile up over the land.

Finishing the job

When a plant or an animal dies, it becomes **detritus**. Detritus is dead material that is breaking down in the soil. Decomposers feed on detritus. They are part of **detritus food chains**.

Putting it back

Decomposers such as earthworms help new prairie plants grow. When they eat, earthworms use some of the nutrients stored in detritus. They put the rest of the nutrients back into the soil through their droppings. Plants can then use the nutrients to make food and to grow.

A detritus food chain

When a plant or an animal, such as this weasel, dies, it becomes dead material in the soil.

Decomposers in the soil, such as this worm, eat the dead material and get some of the energy stored in it. The decomposers then pass some of this energy into the soil through their droppings.

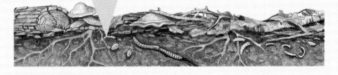

The droppings of decomposers add nutrients to the soil. The nutrients help new plants grow.

Note: The arrows point toward the living things that receive energy.

25

Prairie food webs

Most prairie animals belong to more than one food chain. Each food chain includes plants, a herbivore, and a carnivore. Food chains connect when an animal from one food chain eats plants or animals from another food chain. When two or more food chains connect, they form a **food web**. There can be many plants and animals in a food web.

Minks live along the banks of prairie streams. They belong to many prairie food webs. Minks eat rabbits, ground squirrels, voles, and fish. They are eaten by many animals, as well. Foxes, owls, wolves, bobcats, and hawks eat minks.

A prairie food web
This diagram shows a prairie food web. The arrows point toward the living things that are receiving energy.

Owls eat mice and prairie dogs.

Foxes eat mice and prairie dogs.

Mice eat grasses and parts of flowering plants.

flowering plants

Prairie dogs eat grasses and parts of flowering plants.

grasses

Prairies at risk

Wild prairie land once covered almost all of central North America. Today, only a few large areas of wild prairie land remain. The greatest threat to prairies is the creation of farms. The soil in prairies is **fertile**, or full of nutrients. Fertile soil is good for growing crops, but many farmers grow the same types of crops in an area year after year. Growing one type of crop uses up the nutrients in the soil. Crops also have short roots, whereas **native** plants in prairies have long roots. Long roots hold the soil in place, but short roots do not. When crops replace prairie plants, much of the soil blows away.

Damaging prairie lands

Ranchers let their cattle **graze**, or feed, on prairie lands. The cattle often eat the native plants faster than the plants can grow! Cattle also have sharp hooves, which crush the soil. If cattle are grazed in a prairie for too long, the native plants stop growing. Eventually, the prairie land turns into a **desert**.

As more people move into prairie lands, they build cities, factories, and farms that leave prairie animals with nowhere to live or find food.

29

Protecting prairies

Prairie lands can still be saved! Many people are working to protect these areas. Some prairie lands have been turned into **preserves**, or areas that are protected by a government. Many **conservation groups** are concentrating on turning farmed areas back into prairies. They buy farms that were once prairies and plant the seeds of native prairie plants on the land. As the native plants grow, prairie animals slowly return to the grasslands.

Protecting prairie lands will ensure that many animals have safe places to live.

Share what you know!

Many people do not know that prairie lands are in danger. You can help save prairies by spreading the word! Ask your teacher if your class can create a magazine about the prairies and the many animals that live there. You can write a story about the bison and how they almost disappeared from prairie grasslands. Paint a picture of your own prairie dog town to let people know about these interesting animals. Once your magazine is finished, pass it around to the other classes in your school. When more people know about prairies, there will be more people working to save them!

By creating artwork about your favorite prairie animals, you can help save the animals and have fun, too!

Our Prairie

Volume 1

Prairie Art Show
page 4

Learn how YOU can help
page 10

Published by the Junior Elementary School Third Grade Students

Glossary

Note: Boldfaced words that are defined in the text may not appear in the glossary.

conservation group A group of people whose members work to protect natural areas

desert A dry area of land where very few plants grow

energy The power living things get from food that helps them move, grow, and stay healthy

native Plants that have always lived in a particular place or area

nutrients Substances in food that help living things grow and stay healthy

oxygen A gas needed by animals to breathe that is part of air

pigment A natural color found in plants or animals

population The total number of a type of plant or animal living in a certain place

Index

32

1 2 3 4 5 6 7 8 9 0 Printed in the U.S.A. 4 3 2 1 0 9 8 7 6 5